Introduction

There are many books to help learn how to read Arabic. This book is different in three main ways:

1. We teach primarily with the **beginning forms** of the letters. Most Arabic books teach the ending form first but letters are most often seen as their beginning or middle forms (which are often identical). It's also quite easy to decipher an ending form if you know its beginning form but the opposite is often not true.

2. We use **mnemonic devices**, imagery, or stories to help you remember the letter shapes.

3. Since Arabic letters require vowels (diacritics) for reading, we teach the **letters with vowels** right up front.

We hope this approach simplifies and hastens your journey towards reading Arabic!

I would like to offer special thanks to Dr. Ilhan Cagri, a doctor of Linguistics from the University of Maryland, who pioneered the underpinnings of this teaching method. Also a special thanks to Imam Muhammad al-Asi who graciously offered his time to help me complete work.

i

أَ

Arabic Vowels

أُء

إِ

ا
Alif

The *Alif* is the first letter of the Arabic alphabet but it has no sound on its own.

Like all Arabic letters, we need a vowel marking to pronounce it.

Note: The Alif actually has an extra shape called a Hamza on it in order to be pronounced. We will talk about that in a few pages.

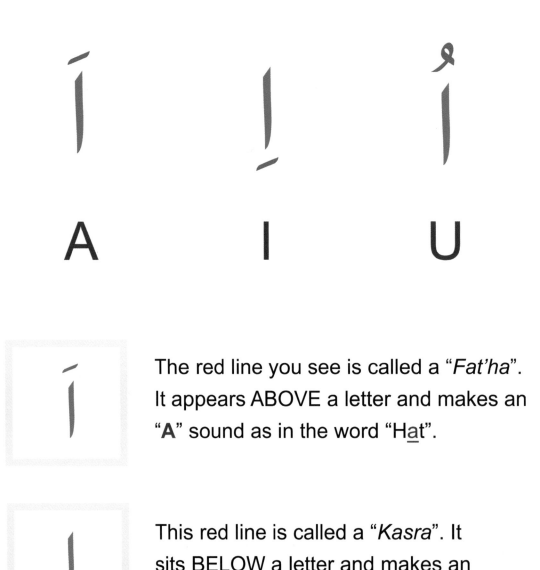

A   I   U

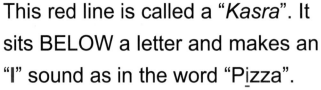

The red line you see is called a "*Fat'ha*". It appears ABOVE a letter and makes an "**A**" sound as in the word "H<u>a</u>t".

This red line is called a "*Kasra*". It sits BELOW a letter and makes an "**I**" sound as in the word "P<u>i</u>zza".

This red curl is called a "Dhamma". It sits ABOVE a letter and makes an "**U**" sound as in the word S<u>u</u>shi.

3

In this book we will try to give you images to help you remember your letters and sounds. Here are some that can help you remember your vowels.

The "a" sound is like a **hat** on *top* of a letter so it makes an "a" sound.

"a" like hat

The "i" sound is like **feet** that are *below* a letter. You can think of feet to remember the sound it makes.

"i" like pizza

The "U/Oo" sound looks like a **monkey's tail** and a monkey says "Oo Oo Oo"!

"u" like sushi

SHORT VOWEL PRACTICE

Let's practice your short vowels by reading the lines below one and at time. Remember, Arabic is read from right to left so remember to **START HERE:**

 أَ   اِ   أُ   اِ   أُ   اُ

أَ   اِ   اِ   اِ   أُ   اِ

اِ   أُ   أُ   اِ   اِ   اُ

أُ   اِ   أُ   اِ   أُ   أَ

ONE MORE THING

There is one more little detail you need to learn.

When the *Alif* is combined with a short vowel, we add a little shape called a *"Hamza"* that looks like a backwards 2. This sits on top of the Alif if it is an "A" or "U", and under the Alif for an "I".

So when you see an Alif with a short vowel on it, it will also have a Hamza like this:

A   I   U

Note: The hamza can sit on other letters too and even float on its own, but we will learn about this later

READING PRACTICE: ALIF WITH HAMZA AND SHORT VOWELS

إ   ا   أُ   إ   أُ   إ   أ

أُ   ا   أُ   إ   أ   إ   أ   ا

أُ   ا   أ   إ   أ   إ   أُ

إ   أ   أُ   إ   أ   إ   أُ   ا

In English vowels appear as letters in a word. But in Arabic, the short vowels sit atop or beneath a letter. Let's look at some examples of english words written with Arabic vowels.

Ba → B́

Ti → Ṯ

Nu → Ń

DaDa → D́D́

TaBu → T́B́

READING PRACTICE: ARABIC VOWELS ON ENGLISH LETTERS

Ǩ   H   J́   Ťh   T̨   B́

Ǵ   Śh   S̨   Ž   R̨   D́

Ň   Ḿ   L̨   Ǩ   Q́   F́

Ȟ   N̨   J́   Y̌   W̨   H́

Chapter 1

B

This letter is called "*Ba*" and makes a **B** sound.

HOW YOU CAN REMEMBER IT

The **B**a has a dot on the **B**ottom

READING WITH VOWELS

Now let's combine it with a vowel

Bu   **Bi**   **Ba**

T

This letter is called "*ta*" and makes a **T** sound.

HOW YOU CAN REMEMBER IT

The **T**a has **T**wo dots on **T**op.

Tu   Ti   Ta

12

Th

This letter is called "*tha*" and makes a **Th** sound as in the word "<u>th</u>ree".

HOW YOU CAN REMEMBER IT

The **Th**a has **Th**ree dots.

Thu   **Thi**   **Tha**

N

This letter is called "*noon*" and makes an **N** sound.

The dot on top is like the sun which is overhead at **N**oon

Nu

Ni

Na

Y

This letter is called *"ya"* and makes a **Y** sound as in Yak and Bay.

HOW YOU CAN REMEMBER IT

The *ya* has two dots beneath it like a skateboard. A skateboarder says "**Yeah** dude!"

Yu   Yi   Ya

 **B**a - One dot on the Bottom

 **T**a - Two dots on Top

 **Th**a - Three dots on top

 **Na** - One dot on top

 **Y**a - Two dots on the Bottom

Note: When a letter is at the end of a word it's written in a "Fancy" way to make the words look nice. We'll learn about this later.

LETTER PRACTICE 1

بَ بُ بَ بُ بِ بُ بِ بَ

تَ تُ تَ تِ تُ تُ تِ تَ

ثَ ثُ ثِ ثُ ثَ ثُ ثِ ثَ

نَ نُ نُ نِ نَ نُ نِ نَ

يُ يَ يُ يَ يِ يُ يِ يَ

بُ نَ ثُ أَ نُ ثُ ثَ يَ
        تِ

ثَ بِ يِ نَ بُ تَ ثُ
تُ

Arabic script connects letters together much like cursive. Letters that end with a line extending left (like a ـبـ) will connect to the next letter.

Those that don't (like an ا) are "shy" and won't connect to the letter after them.

READING WORDS WITH VOWELS

 Aba

 Ba-a

 Bata

 Batu

THE SUKOON

The Sukoon sits on top of a letter and creates a stop on that letter sound. So instead of "Ba" you just say the "B" sound as in the word "Ta<u>b</u>".

HOW YOU CAN REMEMBER IT

The sukoon is like a STOP sign. When you see it, STOP on the letter.

READING WORDS WITH VOWELS

 Aba

 Ab

 Bata

 Bat

19

READING PRACTICE 1

To read Arabic words, you just have to read each letter with each sound, making sure to stop on any sukoons.

Try reading these simple english words:

REMEMBER TO READ RIGHT TO LEFT!

If you read, "Bat", "Eat", and "Nat", congrats! You are reading Arabic!

Chapter 2

H

This letter is called "*Ha*" and makes a hard **H** sound, like the sound you make when frosting up a window on a cold day.

HOW YOU CAN REMEMBER IT

The **Ha** has a clean sound so it has no dots

READING WITH VOWELS

Now let's combine it with vowels

Hu   Hi   Ha

J

This letter is called "*Jeem*" and makes a **J** sound.

The *Jeem* is a Ha with a dot on the bottom

Now let's combine it with vowels

Ju   Ji   Ja

Kh

This letter is called "*Kha*" and makes a **Kh** sound as in the name "**Kh**alid".

HOW YOU CAN REMEMBER IT

The *Kha* scratches the **top** of your mouth when you say it. Just like the dot on **top**.

READING WITH VOWELS

Now let's combine it with vowels

Khu

Khi

Kha

24

 **J**a - A *Ha* with a dot underneath

 **H**a - No dots

 **Kh**a - A *Ha* with a dot on top

Notice: These letters have very fancy swirls if they are at the end of a word.

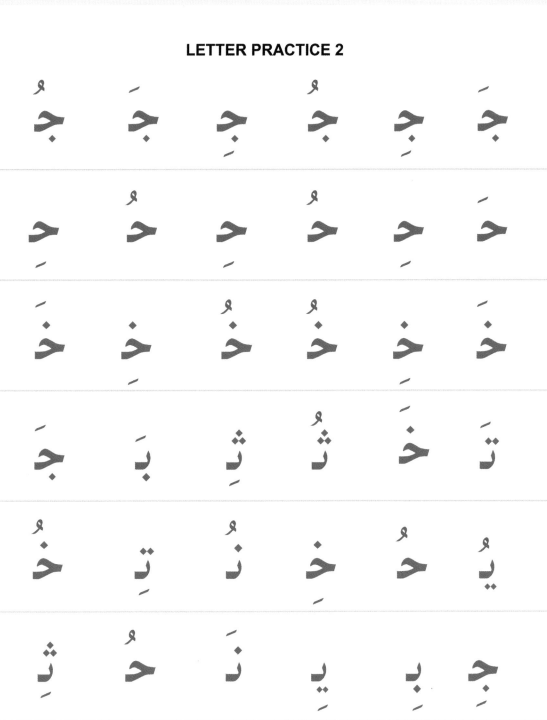

Now that you know more letters, lets see if you can read the english words below!

Chapter 3

ف

ق

م

ف

ق

F

This letter is called "Fa" and makes an **F** sound.

HOW YOU CAN REMEMBER IT

The **F**a looks like a **F**ish that you are giving **F**ish **F**ood to.

READING WITH VOWELS

Now let's combine it with vowels

Fu

Fi

Fa

Q

This letter is called "Qaf" and makes a **Q** sound as in the word Qur'an.

HOW YOU CAN REMEMBER IT

Two dots is too much food and makes the fish make a "Q" sound because it's choking!

READING WITH VOWELS

Now let's combine it with vowels

Qu   Qi   Qa

30

M

This letter is called "Meem" and makes an **M** sound.

HOW YOU CAN REMEMBER IT

The **M**eem looks like a **M**ouse

READING WITH VOWELS

Now let's combine it with vowels

Mu   **Mi**   **Ma**

31

   **F**a - A fish eating food

        Qa - Too much food
        makes the fish choke

   **M**a - looks like a **m**ouse   م

فَ	فُ	فِ	فُ	فِ	فَ
قِ	قُ	قَ	قُ	قَ	قَ
مَ	مِ	مُ	مُ	مِ	مَ
قُ	مِ	فُ	بُ	فِ	جَ
مُ	فِ	إِ	حُ	تَ	جُ
نُ	يُ	مَ	جَ	ثُ	قَ
يِ	قُ	فُ	بِ	خُ	مِ

READING PRACTICE 3

Try to read these English words with the new letters you learned!

Chapter 4

ز

د

و

ذ

ر

D

This letter is called "*Daal*" and makes a **D** sound.

The **D**aal looks like the mouth of a **D**uck

Now let's combine it with vowels

Du　　　　**Di**　　　　**Da**

36

Dh

This letter is called "*Dhaal*" and makes a **Dh** sound like <u>Th</u>at and <u>Th</u>is.

HOW YOU CAN REMEMBER IT

A Daal with a dot is a Dhaal

READING WITH VOWELS

Now let's combine it with vowels

Dhu   **Dhi**   **Dha**

R

This letter is called "*Ra*" and makes a rolled **R** sound.

The **R**a is **R**ound

Now let's combine it with vowels

Ru   Ri   Ra

Z

This letter is called "*Za*" and makes a **Z** sound.

HOW YOU CAN REMEMBER IT

A Ra with a dot is a Za

READING WITH VOWELS

Now let's combine it with vowels

Zu	**Zi**	**Za**

و

W

This letter is called "Wow" and makes a **W** sound.

HOW YOU CAN REMEMBER IT

The Wow looks like a BIG Dhamma, so when people see it they say **W**OW!

READING WITH VOWELS

Now let's combine it with vowels

وُ	وِ	وَ
Wu	Wi	Wa

 **D**a - like the mouth of a **D**uck

 **Dh**a - A Da with a dot on top

 **R**a - The **R**a is **R**ound

 **Z**a - A Ra with a dot on top

 **W**a - A big Dhamma

LETTER PRACTICE 4

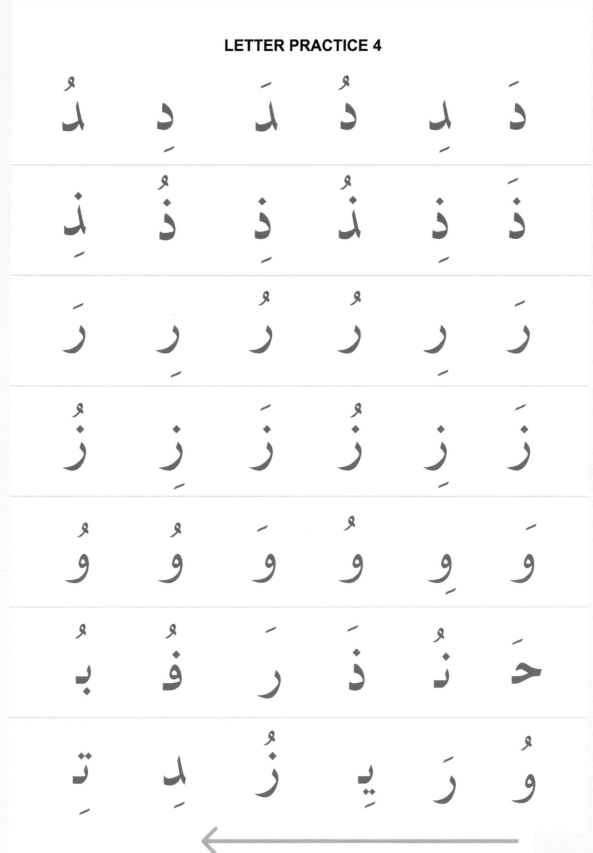

دَ	دِ	دُ	دَ	دِ	دُ
ذَ	ذِ	ذُ	ذِ	ذُ	ذِ
رَ	رِ	رُ	رُ	رِ	رَ
زَ	زِ	زُ	زُ	زِ	زُ
وَ	وِ	وُ	وَ	وُ	وُ
حَ	نُ	ذَ	رَ	فُ	بُ
وُ	يِ	رَ	زُ	دِ	تِ

SHY LETTERS

All Arabic letters can connect to the letter on their right. However, six letters are "Shy" and do not connect on their left. Here are the six shy letters:

HOW YOU CAN REMEMBER IT

The shy letters do not end in a straight line pointing left like the other letters, so they don't connect to their left.

In the example below, notice how the Daal connects to its *right*, but not to its *left*:

BaD

DaB

READING PRACTICE 4

Here's some more English words. See if you can read them!

Chapter 5

س

سـ

ص

ظ

صـ

ش

ض

ش

ض

ط

S

This letter is called "*Seen*" and makes an **S** sound.

HOW YOU CAN REMEMBER IT

The **S**een looks like the waves of the **S**ea

Su   Si   Sa

Sh

This letter is called "*Sheen*" and makes a **Sh** sound.

A *Seen* with 3 dots on top is a *Sheen*

Shu   **Shi**   **Sha**

Ṭ

This letter is called "*Taa*" and makes a heavy **T** sound.

HOW YOU CAN REMEMBER IT

The **T**aw has a **T**all line

READING WITH VOWELS

Now let's combine it with vowels

Ṭu   Ṭi   Ṭa

48

Ḍh

This letter is called "*Dhaa*" and makes a heavy **Dh** sound.

HOW YOU CAN REMEMBER IT

A Taw with a dot on top is a Dhaa

READING WITH VOWELS

Now let's combine it with vowels

Dhu

Dhi

Dha

49

Ṣ

This letter is called "*Sawd*" and makes a heavy **S** sound.

The **S**awd is **S**ad 😢 because unlike his tall brother his line is very **S**mall

Now let's combine it with vowels

Ṣu   Ṣi   Ṣa

Ḍ

This letter is called "*Dawd*" and makes a heavy **D** sound.

HOW YOU CAN REMEMBER IT

A Sawd with a dot is a Dawd

READING WITH VOWELS

Now let's combine it with vowels

Ḍu Ḍi Ḍa

PRONOUNCING HEAVY LETTERS

Heavy letters are pronounced by rounding & puckering your lips before you make the sound.

For example, try saying "*sa*", then try saying it while keeping your lips puckered to make the sound for *"Saad"*. Puckering your lips makes the letter sound **heavy**.

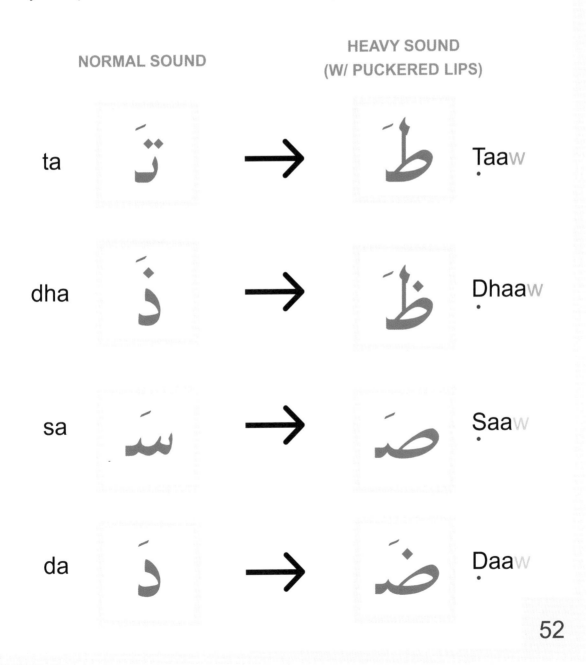

NORMAL SOUND		HEAVY SOUND (W/ PUCKERED LIPS)
ta	→	Ṭaaw
dha	→	Ḍhaaw
sa	→	Ṣaaw
da	→	Ḍaaw

 **S**a - like the waves of the sea

 **Sh**a - *Seen* with 3 dots on top

 **Ṣ**aa - Small line

 **Ḍ**aa - *Saad* with one dot on top

 **Ṭ**aa - Tall line

 **Dha**a - *Ta* with one dot on top

سَ شُ سِ سَ سُ شَ سُ سْ

شَ سِ سُ سَ سِ شُ شَ سِ

صَ ضُ صَ ضِ ضَ صُ صَ صُ

طَ ظُ طَ ظُ طَ ظِ طُ

سُ تَ دُ إِ ضِ ظُ

شَ ثُ طَ فَ صُ نُ

وِ خُ ضِ سُ طَ قَ

READING PRACTICE 5

Try to read these words in Arabic.

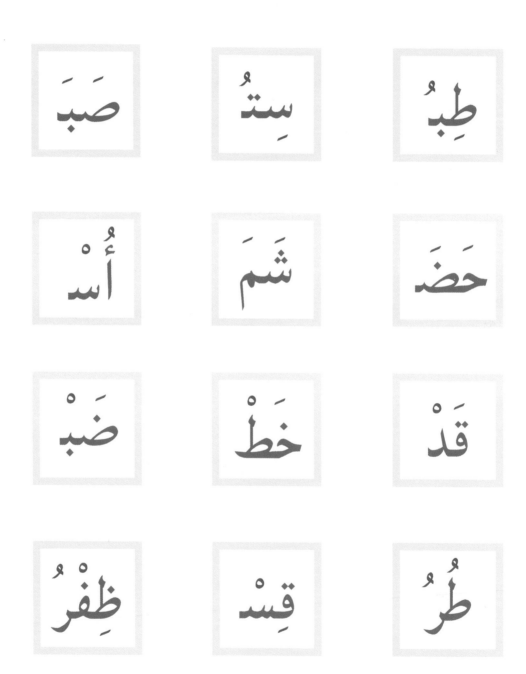

Chapter 6

K

This letter is called "*Kaaf*" and makes a **K** sound.

HOW YOU CAN REMEMBER IT

The **K**aaf looks like a "**K**" without the line on the left.

READING WITH VOWELS

Now let's combine it with vowels

Ku   Ki   Ka

L

This letter is called "*Laam*" and makes an **L** sound.

HOW YOU CAN REMEMBER IT

The **L**aam looks like a backwards "**L**"

READING WITH VOWELS

Now let's combine it with vowels

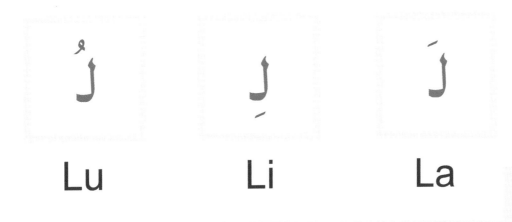

Lu   Li   La

 **K**a - The ending form has a mini *Kaf* inside what looks like a Laam

 **L**a - a backwards L

 We have already learned the *Alif*. You can tell it's an *Alif* because it does not connect to the left like the *Laam.*

"Laa" - When you put an *Alif* after a *Laam* it spells "Laa". The Laa can be written in these three fancy ways.

كُ	كَ	كُ	كُ	كِ	كَ
لَ	لُ	لُ	لِ	لَ	
أَ	كِ	أُ	أُ	أَ	
لُ	كَ	ظُ	بِ	جَ	
دُ	ضِ	لَا	زُ	تَ	لُ
يِ	صُ	كَ	ثُ	ظِ	شَ
نُ	ذِ	سُ	خُ	كَ	رِ

READING PRACTICE 6

أَكَلَ	كَلِمَ	كَلْبُ
إِمْشِ	مَلَك	لَطَمَ
وَلَدَ	سَمَك	كَفَرَ
جَلَسَ	أَلْ	حَجَرُ

Chapter 7

'A

This letter is called 'Ayn and makes an 'A sound from the back of the throat. It's the same sound that starts the name *'Abdullah.*

Now let's combine it with vowels

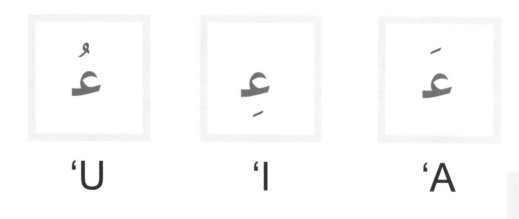

| 'U | 'I | 'A |

Gh

This letter is called "Ghayn" and makes a Gh sound as in the word *Baghdad*.

HOW YOU CAN REMEMBER IT

An 'Ayn with a dot becomes a Ghayn

READING WITH VOWELS

Now let's combine it with vowels

Ghu

Ghi

Gha

This letter is called "ha" and makes a soft h sound as in the word <u>h</u>at. On the next page you will see that the "ha" can be written in five different ways!

HOW YOU CAN REMEMBER IT

The ha is funny because it can be written in so many ways. So we laugh **ha ha ha**!

READING WITH VOWELS

Now let's combine it with vowels

hu   hi   ha

These letters have different ways to write them depending on where they are in a word.

'A - The 'Ayn and Ghayn have 4 different forms

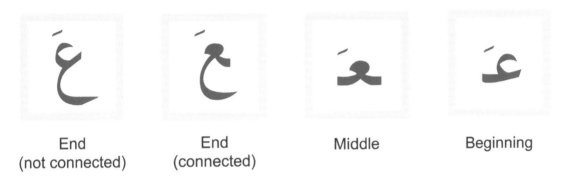

| End (not connected) | End (connected) | Middle | Beginning |

Gha - same as the 'Ayn but with a dot on top

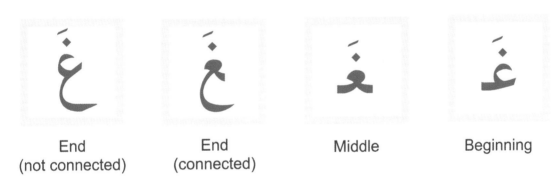

| End (not connected) | End (connected) | Middle | Beginning |

ha - Believe it or not, these are all the letter *ha*!

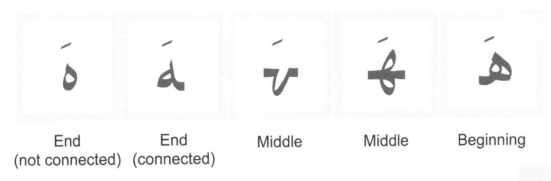

| End (not connected) | End (connected) | Middle | Middle | Beginning |

LETTER PRACTICE 7

عُ	عَ	عِ	عُ	عِ	عَ
غُ	غَ	غِ	غُ	غِ	غَ
هُ	ہِ	هَ	هُ	هِ	هَ
غُ	هَ	غُ	صُ تَ	عَ	
ظُ	جَ	إِ جِ	دُ	هَ	شَ
نُ	هَ	بَ طُ	هُ	غِ	
شُ	طَ	يِ عُ	حُ	ذِ	

READING PRACTICE 7

سَمِعَ	غَرِقَ	عُبِرَ
جَمَعَ	نَهَرَ	هَلَكَ
غَمَزَ	هَرَبَ	دَهَسَ
قَلَمَ	عُمِرُ	غُلَبَ

Chapter 8

The "Hamza" looks like a miniature 'Ayn and takes the sound of the short vowel above or under it.

No matter what letter it is on, if you see a Hamza, JUST pronounce the short vowel that is above or below it.

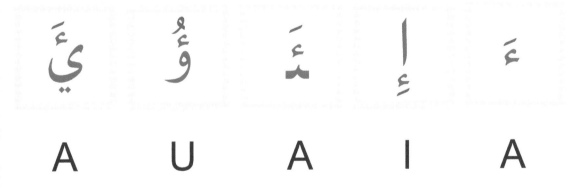

T / h

This is called a "Ta marbuta" and appears at the end of feminine words. Notice the two dots on top just like the Ta (ت) that you already know.

It makes a **T** sound unless you are stopping on the word, as in the end of a sentence. Then it makes a soft **h** sound as in the name Fatimah.

Tu　　　　Ti　　　　Ta

Ban	Bin	Bun

If the vowel at the end of a word is doubled, it adds an "**N**" sound. For the double Fat-ha, we also put an Alif after it that is not pronounced.

بَ	Ba	بًا	Ban
فِ	Fi	فٍ	Fin
تُ	Tu	تٌ	Tun

THE ARABIC ALPHABET - BEGINNING FORMS

🎉 **Congratulations!** 🎉

If you can read the above, you are now
ready to read Arabic!

THE ARABIC ALPHABET - FANCY ENDINGS

When Arabic letters are at the end of a word they are written in a more fancy way so the word looks nice.
Try to recognize the letters in their fancy ending form:

Hint: If you get confused, check the previous page.

READING WITH FANCY FORMS

We've been reading without the fancy endng forms.
Let's see what happens when the last letter uses its
fancy ending.

Try reading these simple English words:

It is easy to mix up letters that can look similar. Try reading these lines to practice distinguishing between the letters!

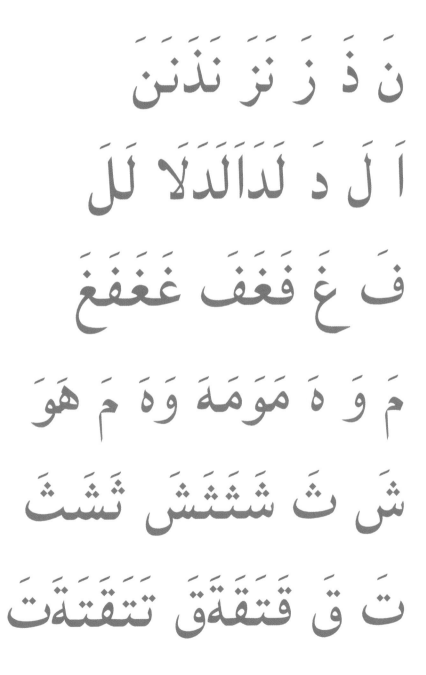

 نَ ذَ زَ نَزَ نَذَنن

اَ لَ دَ لَدَالَدَلَا لَل

فَ غَ فَغَف غَغَفَغ

مَ وَ ةَ مَوَمَة وَةَ مَ هَوَ

شَ ثَ شَثَشَ ثَشَثَشَ

تَ قَ قَتَقَةَقَ تَتَقَتَةَت

READING PRACTICE 8

إِسْمَ	غَرْبُ	نَفْسٍ
أَهْلاً	عَصْرٍ	نَهْرُ
يَدْعُ	فِكْرُ	أَبُ
حَمِدَ	بَعْثُ	سِتْرًا

ال

بِي

ىٰ

Chapter 9

بُو

بَا

THE LONG VOWELS (MADD ṬABEE'EE)

Each short vowel has a special letter that - if placed after it without a vowel of its own - makes the vowel sound longer. These are called the long vowels.

The **Alif** extends the **Fat-ha** into a long **Aaaa** sound.
An extending *Alif* can also be written small and floating.

| Ba | Baa | Baa |

The **Ya** extends the **Kasra** into a long "**Ee**" sound.
An extending *Ya* can also be written like this: ـــ

| Bi | Bee | Behee |

The **Wow** extends the **Dhamma** into an "**oo**" sound.
An extending *Wow* can also be written small.

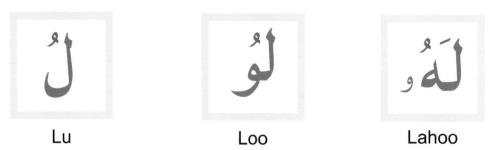

| Lu | Loo | Lahoo |

THE ALIF MAQSURA

This letter looks like a *Ya* without the dots and has a small Alif on top of it. Although it looks like a *Ya*, it's actually an Alif and simply extends the "a" sound before it - just like an Alif.

Musaa

Aqsaa

Mashaa

'Eesaa

THE SHADDAH

Earlier we learned how to extend our vowels. In Arabic, you can also extend consonants. This is called a *"Shaddah"* and sits on top of a letter. When a Shaddah is on a letter you hold the letter sound for twice as long as normal.

Note if you have a Shaddah and Kesra, the Kesra can move from below the letter to just below the Shaddah!

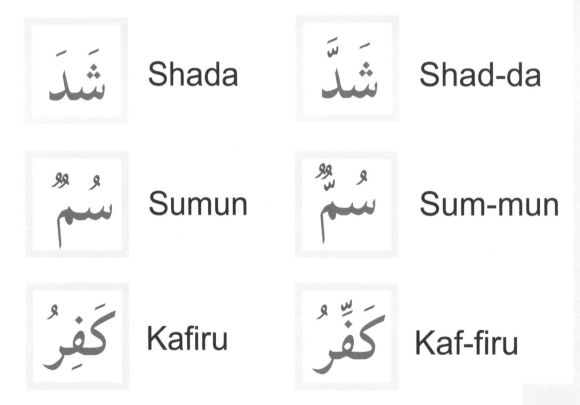

شَدَ	Shada	شَدَّ	Shad-da
سُم	Sumun	سُمَّ	Sum-mun
كَفِرُ	Kafiru	كَفِّرُ	Kaf-firu

READING PRACTICE 9

Try reading these Arabic words!

نُورٌ   كَثِيرٌ

كِتَابٌ   شَرٌّ

سَلَامٌ   أَزْرَقُ

ذَٰلِكَ   قَالَ

شَمْسِ   إِبْنَةِ

سَبَّحَ   ذَاهِبٌ

In English, we can say "the book" and "a book". In Arabic you would say "Al book" and "Bookun".

"Al" (ال) means "**the**" but it's not a separate word. Instead, it connects to the word next to it.

There is no Arabic word for "**a**". Instead, you simply double the vowel at the end of the word (which adds an "n" sound).

Kitaabun

A book

Al kitaabu

The book

When the letter after a Laam has a Shaddah, it's hard to say the Laam so you skip it. For example, in the word above, instead of saying "Al Shamsu" you read it "Ash-shamsu".

HOW YOU CAN REMEMBER IT

The Laam will also have no short vowel on it which is another hint that you can skip it.

Al qamaru

(Pronounce the laam)

Ash-shamsu

(Skip the laam)

الذِّكْرَىٰ	الْفِيلُ	الدَّارُ
السَّمَكُ	الْغَيْبُ	الظَّالِمُ
الْكَهْفُ	التَّوْبَةُ	الزَّكَاةُ
الرَّبُّ	الطَّيْرُ	الْوَلَدُ
الْبَقَرَةُ	الشُّكْرُ	النُّورُ
الصَّبْرُ	الثُّلُثُ	الْعَمَلُ
الضَّالِينَ	الْأَسَدُ	اللَّيْلُ

Chapter 10

When a *Laam* is before a *Jeem*, *Ha*, *Kha*, *Meem*, or *ha* it can sit on top of the letter.

Al Jamalu

=

Al Jamalu

(The *laam* sits on the *jeem*)

Al Masjidu

=

Al Masjidu

(The *laam* sits on the *meem*)

Lahum

=

Lahum

(The *laam* sits on the *ha*)

When a *Jeem*, *Ha*, or *Kha* is before another *Jeem*, *Ha*, or *Kha*, it can be stacked on top.

 =

Hajrun

Hajrun
(Ha on top of the Jeem)

 =

Khajalun

Khajalun
(Kha on top of the Jeem)

 =

Rajaha

Rajaha
(Jeem on top of the Ha)

 When a Ba, Ta, Tha, Noon or Ya, is before a *Jeem*, *Ha*, or *Kha* it can combine into a fancy shape.

Bahrun = Bahrun
(Ba combined with Ha)

Yajidu = Yajidu
(Ya combined with Jeem)

Najmun = Najmun
(Noon combined with Jeem)

When a *Ba*, *Ta*, or *Tha*, *Noon*, or *Ya* is before a *Meem*, it can sit on top in a fancy way.

 =

Bimaa

Bimaa

(Ba on top of the Meem)

 =

Thamanan

Thamanan

(Tha on top of the Meem)

 =

Yammun

Yammun

(Ya on top of the Meem)

90

READING PRACTICE 10: ARABIC SENTENCES

Congratulations! Believe it or not you can now read Arabic! Try reading these sentences!

رَأَيْتُ السَّفِينَةَ فِي بَحْرٍ.

وَلَهُمْ نَجْمٌ سَاطِعٌ.

زُرْتُ الْمَسْجِدَ الْأَقْصَى.

رَكِبْتُ الْجَمَلَ فِي الصَّحْرَاءِ.

ذِي اَنْدْ

The End

Special thanks to my first grade Arabic studends - Alio, Farah, Leyann, Malik, Noorah, Safia, Salim, Sophia, Yasamin, Zafar, and Zoeb - whose energy and creativity were instrumental to the development of this work.

Printed in Great Britain
by Amazon

42757706R00055